SUMMARY GUIDE:

Building A StoryBrand

Clarify Your Message So Customers Will Listen by Donald Miller

The Mindset Warrior Summary Guide

by The Mindset Warrior

D1366347

Table of Contents

Hi there! Be Sure to Stick Around to the End for a FREE BONUS.

My gift to you; as a special thank you for purchasing this book.

-The Mindset Warrior

MW Summary Guide Disclaimer

Introduction

In this Mindset Warrior Summary Guide we cover the main topics discussed in "Building A StoryBrand". This book is intended to supplement your reading and be an easy reference guide. You are encouraged to purchase the original book if you have not already.

The difference between this guide and the actual book is that we don't go into the lengthy stories and repetition that most books often do. Instead, we share each principle, explain its reasoning, and then provide advice on how you can apply each to your own marketing.

As I always say, the original books are great to read because they provide a lot of examples. This repetition can help to embed the lessons into your psyche. That being said, stripping these lessons down to there core will help you to focus on the things that really matter. As I'm sure we can agree, time is also very valuable. I am all about maximizing time.

The Mindset Warrior summaries are here to support your journey toward a resilient mindset. **www.mindsetwarrior.com**

Setting The Stage

"Building A StoryBrand" is all about designing your branding and marketing message in a way that will lead to more conversions.

Storytelling has become a more popular topic in the marketing space in recent years due to the fact that customers are being bombarded with more and more messages daily. With that being the case, the challenge of how do to keep their attention, becomes even more of a tough area to navigate.

It is said that the average person sees about 3,000 marketing message a day.

Storytelling for persuasion isn't a completely new phenomena, but specifically structuring our marketing around it is a more recent one.

The author, Donald Miller spends the entire book breaking down his 7 part framework for building the customer's story.

He cultivated his messaging framework through studying stories in various different mediums—from novels to movies to theater. He then applied what he had learned in his own writings, and now he has gone on to consult with many different companies to effectively craft their branding and marketing messages.

This is the first book I've read on storytelling, and its one worth reading. Let's begin.

SECTION 1 – Where Most Marketing Fails

Chapter 1 – How to Be Seen Heard And Understood

It is easy to blame repeated failed marketing campaigns on the wrong product or product market fit, but that often isn't the culprit. The real culprit is the way the product is talked about.

Donald says that a customer should be able to register what you are offering within 5 seconds of viewing it.

Stories are effective because they help the customer make sense of the message. The brain loves shortcuts, thus the more shortcuts you can give it, the better you'll communicate your message.

Branding Mistake #1

Ignoring how the offer will help the customer survive and thrive.

Branding Mistake #2

Causing our customers to tune us out due to our confusing offer.

Humans have mechanisms built in that encourages us to look for shortcuts in order to conserve energy. Asking the customer to decode your offer is asking for too much.

At its foundation, a story organizes information into:

(a) ambition

(b) defined challenges

(c) a plan to overcome those challenges

When it comes to marketing and branding, think of a story as a guide map for our customer that leads them to our offer as the solution.

Maps offer clarity.

A typical story map identifies the following:

(a) who the hero is

(b) what the hero wants

(c) who/what the hero has to defeat to get what they want

(d) what does the hero risk losing if they do not win

(e) what benefits will the hero get from winning

For the StoryBrand formula, you want to do the same. The hero in our case is our customer.

All of our marketing should focus on some element of this map. This focus will help you to reduce excessive information, and obscure marketing attempts, that often distract from the story. The story is what will ultimately lead to the sale.

Chapter 2 – The SB7 Formula

Chapter 2 introduces the 7 elements of the StoryBrand formula.

After studying movies and novels, Donald discovered that most stories have 7 elements that consistently show up.

The 7 elements are:

(1) a character

(2)the character encounters a problem *(internally, externally, philosophically)*

(3) the character meets a guide

(4) the character is provided a plan by the guide

(5) the guide encourages the character to act

(6) the character acts and succeeds

(7) the character avoids failure

Donald emphasizes that the focus of your marketing should always contain those elements and nothing more. The customer should be able to identify each element at any time.

Forming Our Brand Messaging

(1) map out the story of the customer

(2) using the story, create clear statements for each of the 7 elements of the StoryBrand formula

Doing this will help position your company as the guide. Once complete, your messages should fit on a single sheet of paper.

We'll break down the elements later, and as we do, you'll be forming what Donald calls a BrandScript.

The Grunt Test *(a short framework for messaging)*

You should pass all your marketing efforts through what Donald calls "the grunt test".

Within 5 seconds of being exposed to your marketing material, a prospect should be able to identify 3 things:

(1) what do you offer?

(2) how will it make their life better?

(3) what do they need to do to buy?

NOTE: He calls it a "grunt test" because he says a caveman should be able to say it. If you recall, cavemen are known to have very basic language and to talk with a grunt behind their words.

Chapter 3 – The SB7 Framework

Chapter 3 breaks down each element from the StoryBrand formula even further.

NOTE: Each element will be broken down in detail in chapter 4 - 10, but this is a quick outline.

1. A Character

PRINCIPLE: The customer is the hero, not your brand.

First identify your customer segment, and then figure out what they want.

The hero in every story wants something, and the story is the audience figuring out if the hero will get what they want.

2. Character Has A Problem

PRINCIPLE: Sell the internal problem, not the external one.

There are 3 levels of problems a character will face.

(1) internal

(2) external

(3) philosophical

Identify the 3 levels for your customer, and address them in your marketing message.

3. Character Meets A Guide

PRINCIPLE: Customers are looking for a guide, not another hero.

Many companies try to position themselves as a hero, but you actually compete with your customer when you position your brand as the hero.

We are self serving creatures—more focused on our own success over another.

4. The Guide Gives The Character A Plan

PRINCIPLE: Customers trust a guide with a plan

After you've positioned yourself as a guide, the customer needs to know you have a clear plan for solving their problem.

There are 2 types of plans:

(a) the agreement plan - removes the fear in purchasing by making statements of assurance.

(b) the process plan - removes confusion by telling them how to purchase and how to use your offer.

Combining both of these plans will establish trust and increase the customers confidence.

5. The Guide Calls Them to Action

PRINCIPLE: Customers will not take action unless they are challenged to do so.

As energy conserving as we are, we instinctively are not compelled to take action unless an external force encourages action.

Include a clear call to action in every marketing message.

Two of the most commonly used call to actions are ones that ask for the sale or request a meeting; these are called "direct calls to action", and ones that encourage furthering the relationship; these are called "transitional calls to action".

6. The Plan Helps The Character Avoid Failure

PRINCIPLE: Humans are more compelled to avoid pain than they are to get pleasure.

Just as every plot focuses on what can be gained or lost, your marketing should emphasize what will be gained or lost by not purchasing your offer. Because we are more pain-avoidant, the emphasis should be slightly more on the painful aspects.

7. The Character Succeeds In Overcoming The Problem

PRINCIPLE: Tell people how your brand will change their lives. Don't assume they will know.

Every purchase is made to solve a problem. The customer needs to be reminded of the positive changes they will get from solving their problem.

Remember, if given 2 options, we will instinctively chose the path of least resistance. If we don't see a need to act, or don't feel certain about the path that we should select, we'll often procrastinate, or not choose.

The remainder of the book discusses how to identify your brand message and create a script using the 7 elements.

Donald provides a sheet for you to structure your StoryBrand script using the 7 elements that you can find at: myStoryBrand.com

Donald says that you'll want to create multiple brand scripts. Considering creating one for:

- your overall brand

- each division of the company

- each product within each division

- each customer segment

Remember, simplicity and relevancy is what we are after. With those in place, it becomes much more easier to compel others to take action.

SECTION 2 – Building Your StoryBrand Script

Chapter 4 – A Character

In a story, for a problem to truly exist, there needs to be a character encountering it. This provides the motivation and intrigue to keep the audience's attention.

Find out what your customer wants, and find out how to word your offer in a way that aligns with their want.

Story Gaps

A story gap occurs in every story. Its when there is a gap between the character, and what they want. Highlighting this gap is the essence of marketing. It is your job to place your brand or product in the gap.

From General Ambition to Single Focus

While your company may offer multiple solutions. Donald says that it is important to focus on one solution and become well known for it, so that your marketing does not confuse prospects.

In essence, your overall brand addresses one specific main desire with one specific main solution, and your various products feed off the main specific desire into "sub-desires" along with their solutions.

Choose A Desire Relevant To Their Survival

One of the most effective ways to market, is to have your marketing emphasize some sort of threat to your prospects existence. The drive to exist is at the foundation of living.

NOTE: Existence follows exchange physically, monetarily, and socially.

Here are a few examples of what agitates our survival needs:

- Conserving finances.

- Conserving time/energy

- Building social circle

- Gain status

- Accumulating resources

- Desire to be generous

- Desire for meaning/significance

Keep in mind that each customer should know, and be able to easily articulate exactly what your brand will solve for them.

STEPS

(1) Brainstorm the desires your customer has that you can fulfill

(2) Choose the most compelling one that agitates the need for survival

Chapter 5 – Has A Problem

After entering into the customer story by describing their desire, next you want to increase their interest in your brand by talking about the obstacles in getting their desire. Problems are what keep the customer engaged and interested.

Vilifying The Customer's Problems

In addressing your customer's problems, you want to think in terms of a villain. Using a villain gives focus to the story. In marketing, you should position oyur offer as the solution to defeating the villain.

NOTE: The villain doesn't have to be a person. For example, boredom can be the villain when selling an entertainment product.

Donald's 4 rules for creating your villain:

(1) The villain should be a root source, not an effect. *(for example, don't emphasize the cavity, emphasize sugary foods)*

(2) The villain should be widely recognized as unpleasant

(3) There should only be one villain that you identify in your marketing

(4) The villain should be real; rather than speculative or imagined.

The 3 Levels of Conflict

There are 3 levels of problems that when combined, capture and maintain attention. First, the villain creates an external problem. As a result the customer experiences internal conflict, and with that feels philosophically conflicted in some way.

External

The villain exists to pose a threat. Not until the threat is experienced; leading to the external problem, is it enough for a person to act.

The external problem is often physical.

Internal

People buy due to the frustrating feelings *(internal problems)* they encounter from external problems.

Internal problems are more motivating than external ones.

Oftentimes in movies, this is where the writer brings up the person's past traumas or insecurities, in order to explain their current behavior.

The question that often makes up the internal problem is "Do I have what it takes?"

examples of internal problems = frustration, intimidation, doubt, embarrassment

Philosophical

The philosophical problem explains why solving the problem matters from a broader, more worldly, perspective.

This is where "should" and "deserve" statements come up.

Consider the deeper story that your brand is involved in, and identify how your products help push back against a certain perceived injustice.

The Perfect Brand Promise

Instead of focusing on the product, focus your messaging on the external, internal, and philosophical problems your product solves.

When you synchronize the 3 levels of problems into your brand message, you will pull your customer into your BrandStory.

STEPS

(1) Brainstorm the literal and metaphorical villains your brand*(or product)* stands against

(2) Brainstorm the external problems your brand resolves. Which one represents the majority of your product line/brand?

(3) Brainstorm the internal problems your customer faces. Which one is experienced by the most customers?

(4) Is there a philosophical wrong the brand stands against?

Chapter 6 – Meets A Guide

Characters solving their own problems is not interesting enough to keep attention, there must be a guide involved. Alongside that observation, people often aren't self motivated enough, and they rely on external sources of motivation.

It is common for companies to position themselves as the hero; though they should be positioning themselves as the guide. The guide is the person who has already overcame the customer's problem, as a result, the branding message should not be focused on the company, but rather the customer.

Donald has observed that this simple shift in messaging, dramatically affects response rates.

The 2 Characteristics of A Guide

(a) Empathy

(b) Authority

Communicating Empathy

When you express empathy, you tell the customer that you understand their frustrations, and as a result you gain their trust.

Similar to the popular phrase; "people don't care how much you know until they know how much you care", customers will lose interest if they don't feel you care about them.

Once you've identified their internal problem. Finds areas in your marketing message where you can use phrases like:

- "nobody should have to experience..."

- "like you, we are frustrated by..."

- "we care about your..."

The key to making your messaging convincing is to get the customer to believe you are just like them. When commonality is detected, the human brain tends to shortcut other areas of critique with trust.

NOTE: Commonality can be as simple as a shared taste in music, food, or values.

Demonstrating Authority

Donald outlines 4 ways to demonstrate authority without being "braggy".

(1) Testimonials

(2) Statistics

(3) Awards

(4) Logos from credible sources

Making A Good First Impression

When people meet your company, they want to identify a few things:

- Will you get along?

- Can you help them live a better life?

- Do they want to associate their identity with you?

- Can they trust you?

STEPS

(1) Brainstorm empathetic statements you can make in your messaging so that your customers know you care about their internal problems.

(2) Brainstorm the ways you can demonstrate competence and authority through testimonials, stats, awards you've won, and logos of other companies you've be associated with.

Chapter 7 – Who Gives Them A Plan

At his stage in the journey, we have the customer's interest, but they are not prepared to make a purchase *(aka a commitment)*.

The addition of a plan, removes confusion, fills the story gap the customer must cross, and makes the pursuit seem a lot less intimidating.

Donald says all plans do 1 of the following 2 things:

(a) they clarify how someone can do business with us

(b) they remove the sense of risk somebody might have

Asking for the sale is not enough to compel a person to buy because of their self doubts, past traumas, and overall uncertainty that still lingers in their brain. Your brand plan should be very clear and make the process easy for them to understand and embark on.

Donald has identified two types of plans that are most effective: the process plan and the agreement plan.

The Process Plan

The main purpose of the process plan is to remove confusion. It either describes the steps a customer needs to go through to purchase *("pre-purchase process plan),* or the steps they need to take to use the product after their purchase*("post-purchase process plan)*—you can also combine the two.

Each plan should have between 3 to 6 steps in order to not overwhelm the customer. If more are required, segment them into labeled phases.

The Agreement Plan

The main purpose of an agreement plan is to remove fear. You'll want to create a list of agreements to present to your customers in order to remove their fear of doing business with you.

Other benefits of agreement plans include:

- shared sense of purpose

- increased perception of value

In forming an agreement plan, first list all the concerns a customer may have about your product or service, then counter their concerns with an agreement plan statement.

Naming The Plans

Donald says that giving the plans a compelling title will increase perceived value.

STEPS

(1) Brainstorm the steps a customer would need to take to do business with you; both pre and post purchase, or combine the two.

(2) What fears do your customers have related to the industry? What agreements could you make to alleviate those fears?

(3) What unique values do you share with your customers? Can they be highlighted in the agreement plan?

(4) Brainstorm names for the plan(s) that give off the impression of higher value.

Chapter 8 – And Calls Them To Action

Before the customer can experience the results of your product, they need to be challenged to take action.

A Lack of Belief

Donald says that not asking for the sale translates to the customer as a lack of belief in your product. The more bold; yet appropriate, we are about asking for the sale, the more we display certainty about our product, and as a result our authority increases.

The 2 Types of Calls to Action

There are 2 types of calls to action: direct and transitional. These work together in phases.

Transitional CTA's

These calls to action are for those who aren't ready to buy. These allow you to maintain a relationship with the prospect so that you are not forgotten when the prospect is ready to buy.

examples: free information, samples, free trials, and testimonials

These calls to actions serve 3 main functions:

- establishes your authority

- displays your generosity

- positions you as the guide

Direct CTA's

These calls to action ask for a specific action that will lead to a sale. They should be included at the end of every marketing piece and in multiple places on your website.

examples: schedule an appointment today, buy now, order now, call today, register today

Donald suggests having a *"buy now"* button placed in multiple areas of your website:

- the top right corner

- above the fold *(meaning before they scroll down)*

- in the center

- repeated at various intervals

Donald says that switching back and forth between the two types of calls to action is what will bring success, but we should always make sure we emphasize the direct CTAs more.

STEPS

(1) Brainstorm a list of transitional calls to actions that you can create.

(2) Brainstorm a list of direct calls to action that will resonate with your audience.

Chapter 9 – That Helps Them Avoid Failure

Chapter 9 is about communicating what can be potentially lost *(i.e. the stakes)*, if the prospect does not purchase your offer.

A great way to do this is by foreshadowing the pitfalls of not taking you up on your offer. This opens the story gap, and then your offer is the solution to close it.

Motivated By Potential Loss

Psychology has shown that people tend to overvalue what they have. As a result, anything that poses a threat to what they have will be higher on their radar. This tendency to be more loss-avoidant versus gain-promoting, is known as "prospect theory".

Donald presents a 4 step process by the name of "fear appeal" from the book, "Building Communication Theory". Using this framework, we can effectively craft our messaging to highlight loss.

(1) inform them of their vulnerability to a threat *(ex: statistic)*

(2) explain to them that since they're vulnerable, they should take action to reduce their vulnerability *(in order to not be a part of the statistic)*

(3) specify a call to action that protects them from risk *(the solution/CTA available is our offer)*

(4) challenge them to take the call to action *(the specific steps to take us up on our offer)*

A Healthy Amount of Fear

Its important to avoid over-emphasizing fear. Too much will lead to paralysis, while too little will not be enough to incite action. Chose only a few horrible consequences that you can emphasize in your marketing material.

STEPS

(1) Brainstorm the negative consequences you are helping your customer avoid

(2) Settle on 3 of the best negative consequences from step 1

Chapter 10 – And Ends In A Success

Chapter 10 is about ending the story. You want to emphasize where your offer will take the customer. You want to answer the question: "What will life look like once I succeed?"

Remember, specificity & clarity matters in answering these questions.

Highlighting The Journey

Start by identifying how your customer's life looked before your offer.

- What do they have?

- What are they feeling?

- What is an average day like?

- What is their status?

By first identifying the beginning, you can help the customer see that you understand them, then go on to explain what life will look like after.

How to End The Story for The Customer

The success portion of your StoryBrand Script should address the resolutions to their 3 levels of problems.

How does their life look externally now? *(external problem)*

How do they feel now? *(internal problem)*

How has their achievement positively impacted the world? *(philosophical problem)*

Donald identified 3 ways in which storytellers predominantly end a story. He suggests that we find a way to end our StoryBrand in one of these 3 ways:

(1) the hero wins status

(2) the hero is unified with someone or something that completes them

(3) the hero experiences a self-realization that completes them

Offering status

- offer exclusive access

- create scarcity with a limited time offer

- offer a premium version

- offer identity association

Offering external salvation

- reduce anxiety

- reduced workload

- save time

Offering the ability to reach your potential

- inspiration *(external)*

- acceptance *(internal)*

- transcendence *(philosophical)*

NOTE: Using lifestyle images that show a person happily engaging with your product has been shown to increase responsiveness.

STEP:

Brainstorm how your customer's life will look like after using your product or service.

Chapter 11 – Your Role As Transformation Facilitator

Humans strongly desire transformation. Innately, we have a subconscious awareness that stagnation inhibits survival. If you effectively help a customer transform their lives and/or identity, they will be in-debt to you.

Donald encourages us to answer 2 questions:

- Who does our customer want to become? *(concrete)*

- What is their aspirational identity? *(abstract)*

Defining An Aspirational Identity

What character traits accurately fit with your StoryBrand resolutions?

How does your customer want to be described by their friends?

What figures or metaphors can you use in your marketing material to communicate those characteristics?

Brainstorm answers to those 3 questions, and then incorporate the best ones with the 3 levels of problems you are solving for your customer.

Obsess About The Transformation

Usually after the heroic climax of a story, the storyteller then moves on to affirm the transformation of the hero. This often shows up as the hero revisiting an old familiar environment, or some other contrasting flashback.

Testimonials work very similarly. Your customers need to be told/shown how far they've come, how far they can go, or how far others before them have come.

STEPS

(1) Brainstorm the aspirational identity of your customer *(how do they want to be perceived?)*

(2) Using a "to - from" framework. Identify the aspirational identity that most fits. Then record a "to" *(i.e. prior identity)* and then a "from"*(i.e. post identity)* in your StoryBrand script

SECTION 3 - Implementing Your StoryBrand Script

Chapter 12 – Building A Better Website

The key to a successful website is simplicity.

Donald says that our websites should be in the format of an elevator pitch: clear and concise. You want to reduce any extra words or images that do not clearly add to your messaging.

Through analyzing various websites, Donald has identified 5 elements that should be included on every website.

(1) An offer above the fold *(an offer that can be seen before scrolling)*

The offer should be clear and presented in as few words as possible.

Donald urges that the images and texts above the fold should have at least one of the following criteria:

(a) promise an aspirational identity

(b) promise to solve a problem

(c) a statement of exactly what your company does

(2) Obvious call to action

Donald suggests having a *"buy now"* button placed in multiple areas of your website:

- the top right corner

- above the fold *(meaning before they scroll down)*

- in the center

- repeated at various intervals

The direct CTA button should be different than all the other buttons on the page; especially in brightness.

The transitional calls to action should be on the page too, but in a less obvious color. Donald says placing it next to the direct call to action can sometimes be a good option.

(3) Images of success

Donald suggests including happy people in your images; preferably with you product in hand, at your service spot, or with a representative.

(4) A Breakdown of your core offers

If you have multiple offers, breakdown your offer into two set categories, and have a brand script for each. There should be an option on your main page to go down one path for a certain set of offers, or go down another. Customers need to know clearly that what you offer is for them. Combining multiple offers that vary in their purpose can be confusing.

(5) Very few words

People tend to scan websites. Donald says the most effective websites that he has audited, tend to have 10 sentences or less on one page.

He suggests using a *"read more"* tab at the bottom of the page if you must add more words.

Consider the following:

Can you replace some of your texts with images?

Can you reduce whole paragraphs into 3-4 bullet points?

Can you summarize sentences into small sound bites?

Overall, the key is to make sure everything that appears on your website is derived from some element of your StoryBrand script. If it doesn't, you'll risk confusing the customer.

Chapter 13 – Using StoryBrand to Transform Company Culture

Chapter 13 shifts the focus from customer BrandScripts to employee BrandScripts for better employee management.

Donald introduces the concept of *"the narrative void"*. This is when the company employees lack engagement because there is no story that makes their efforts feel purposeful, or makes unifying amongst each other worthwhile.

"Where there is no plot. There is no productivity" - Donald Miller

The Cost of The Narrative Void

Gallup polls have shown that 1 out of every 5 employee reported being engaged with their work. This observation has revealed billions of dollars in lost productivity. Information overload and social disconnection are said to be the main forces at fault.

Getting Your Team On The Same Page

By introducing a StoryBrand into your company culture, employees can shift the focus from what they can get out of the company to who they will become as a result of being a part of the company.

For example, in the hiring process, HR should walk the prospective employee through the 7 stages of the StoryBrand formula as it pertains to your company; in order to make sure your narrative resonates with them.

When The Mission Comes To Life

Most mission statements fall short because they fail to make the employee a hero. Remember, people appeal to their own self interest first.

Donald introduces the concept of *"thoughtmosphere"*. Its a made up word that describes a mixture of belief and ideas that drive employee behavior.

There are various different ways to create your thoughtmosphere.

One case study improve their thoughtmosphere through:

- video curriculum

- regional meetings

- a national convention

- casual updates from the CEO

- retreats for certain top level execs

- inspirational speakers

- concerts on the beach

These changes shifted their growth from 5% to 30% in less than 3 years.

Getting Your Company On Mission

STEPS

(1) create a StoryBrand script with the leadership team

(2) audit the existing thoughtmosphere

(3) create a StoryBrand script implementation plan

(4) optimize internal communications to support the plan

(5) install a self-sustained team to enhance the culture

Donald explains that the activities in a StoryBrand culture often look similar to those in cultures that do not use it, but the difference is that the StoryBrand culture is unified around a clear and compelling narrative.

Increasing The Employee Value Proposition

Besides raises, there are other ways to keep the team engaged by appealing to their self interest.

Here are a list of ideas:

- opportunities to advance

- receiving recognition

- promoting flexibility

- compensation packages

- organized events.

Remember the team member is the hero, and leadership serves the role as a guide. This is also why it is so important to understand the goals of each prospective employee before highering. The closer you can get to the team member's vision aligning with the company culture, the better efforts you'll get from them, and the happier customers you'll have.

;

Chapter 14 – The StoryBrand Marketing Strategy Roadmap

The final chapter breaks down a series of 5 marketing/messaging efforts to put your BrandScript into action.

First you want to make sure you have your BrandScript, next you want to integrate your BrandScript into your website like discussed in Chapter 12, and finally begin focusing on the 5 activities discussed in this chapter.

(1) Create a one-liner

(2) Create a lead generator and collect email addresses

(3) Create an automated email drip campaign

(4) Collect and tell stories of transformation

(5) Create a system that generates referrals

TASK 1: Create a one-liner

A one liner answers the "what do you do?" question in a way that clarify informs the prospect on how your product or service can enhance their lives.

There are 2 aspects that should be included in your one-liner:

(a) imagination

(b) intrigue

Donald says you can get to those by using a succinct version of the StoryBrand formula.

1) Character - Who is your customer?

2) Problem - What is their problem?

3) Plan - What is your plan to help them?

4) Success - What will their life look like after you help them?

He goes on to explain that the one-liner doesn't have to be one sentence, but it shouldn't be more than 3. We want the statement to be easily repeatable and understandable.

Here is the example he provides in the book.

The Character: Moms

The Problem: Busy schedules

The Plan: Short, meaningful workouts

The Success: Health and renewed energy

One Liner: "We provide busy moms with a short, meaningful workout they can use to stay healthy and have renewed energy."

<u>Ways to use the one-liner:</u>

- Have the entire team memorize the one-liner

    NOTE: Consider putting it on posters, shirts, mugs, etc.

- Include it on your website

- Include it in every marketing material you publish

TASK 2: Create a lead generator and collect email addresses

The best way to grow an email list is through inciting a transitional call to action. These are those calls to action that aren't directly selling anything, but starts the relationship with the prospect. The key here is to offer them something interesting for free. This is known as a "lead magnet".

How to Create an Irresistible Lead Magnet

Donald says that here are 2 guidelines your lead magnet should follow.

(a) provide exceptional value

(b) establish your company as an authority

He has witnessed the following lead magnets to be the most effective:

(a) downloadable guide

(b) online course or webinar

(c) software demonstration or a free trial

(d) free samples

(e) live events

Create a very compelling title for the lead magnet.

Examples of compelling titles provided in the book:

"5 Mistakes People Make with Their First Million Dollars"

"Building Your Dream Home: 10 Things to Get Right Before You Build"—

"Cocktail Club: Learn to Make One New Cocktail Each Month"

Other tips for your lead magnet:

- Be generous in the amount of information you provide

- Place your lead magnet sign up on multiple pages of your website

TASK 3: Create An Automated Email Drip Campaign

Emailing your customers or prospects regularly will keep you top of mind.

An automated email campaign sends pre-written emails on a set interval basis after someone has signed up to your list.

"The idea is that you'll be inviting people into a narrative that leads to a sale even while you sleep." - Donald Miller

Donald offers his own case study where he was sending out mailings, but they weren't being read; yet the simple act of him sending them out increased his revenue.

He said this was because he was reminding his list of the company's existence. While they may not be interested today, tomorrow, or a month from now, they may be interested 6 months from now. And because he was staying on their radar through periodic mailings, they'd likely choose him when they needed his service or product.

<u>When to ask for the sale?</u>

Donald recommends starting with a nurturing campaign. This campaign offers backstory into your product or service, and provides various insights into the customer's problems. Its purpose is to position you as the guide, develop trust, and activate reciprocity. You do not want to ask for a sale until the end of this sequence; anywhere from 3-4 emails.

Crafting A Nurturing Email

Nurturing emails should offer helpful advice. Donald has a formula he uses for them.

(1) Talk about a problem

(2) Explain the plan to solve the problem

(3) Describe how life will look once the problem is solved

(4) Include a P.S.

NOTE: You want to email at least once a week.

The Offer & Call to Action Email

After 3-4 nurturing emails, you want to send your offer. Donald warns that it is important to be direct in order to communicate confidence in your offer.

His formula for these emails is:

(1) Talk about a problem

(2) Explain the plan to solve the problem

(3) Describe how life will look once the problem is solved

(4) Offer a direct call to action

(5) Include a P.S.

NOTE: Donald recommends MailChimp for smaller lists, and InfusionSoft for larger lists. I personally use and recommend GetResponse. They offer the most features along with segmentation for a great price.

TASK 4: Collect & Tell Stories of Transformation

Transformation is a core human drive. By highlighting transformations we grab and keep our audiences attention. Customer testimonials are the best ways to do this. Part of the sales process is raising certainty. By seeing that someone else has gone before us and had success, the customer gains more trust in the offer.

Donald warns that when asking for testimonials its important to ask questions or make requests as to what should be included, otherwise you might get over-flattering responses that don't answer prospects concerns, and that seem inflated.

Donald compiled 5 questions to help you collect compelling testimonials:

1.What was the problem you were having before you discovered our product?

2.What did the frustration feel like as you tried to solve that problem?

3.What was different about our product?

4.Take us to the moment when you realized our product was actually working to solve your problem.

5.Tell us what life looks like now that your problem is solved or being solved.

Use testimonials in your emails, promotional videos, speeches, interviews, and live events.

TASK 5: Create a System That Generates Referrals

You want to create a system that incentives happy customers to tell their friends. Many businesses skip this step, but its one of the best cost savings in business.

In this section Donald walks us through a step by step process to create a referral system.

(1) Identify your existing fanatical customers

These will be customers who have frequently bought from you.

(2) Give them a reason to spread the word

If you make it a chore for them to tell their friends, they likely won't do it. Create a PDF, video, or text template that makes the process easy for them.

(3) Offer a reward

A reward can be a discount, a free ticket to an event, or a percentage off commission for each person who is referred and then purchases.

Automating the Referral System

Consider creating an automated referral system for the customers you've deemed most valuable and satisfied.

GIVEAWAY

I've taken chapter 7 of the summary and expanded it with various

tips and strategies from the other chapters of the book and

turned it into a cheatsheet for your quick reference. Use this to

prepare your StoryBrand script.

You can download the PDF here:

http://mindsetwarrior.com/sb7-formula-opt

Conclusion

I really enjoyed writing this "Creating A StoryBrand" summary. Donald did a fantastic job of creating a framework around storytelling. I hope you found this summary useful. I did my best to breakdown everything I could in a way that'll be easy to review at a glance. Similarly, I've done summaries on several sales books that you might be interested in. Now that you have the formula for your branding and marketing, you'll have to sell it. I did a summary on "SPIN Selling" by Neil Rackham", on how to ask the right questions in order to close deals, and another summary on "Fanatical Prospecting by Jeb Blount", on how to get and maintain your prospects attention. You can find both of those summaries at http://mindsetwarrior.com/summary-guides Keep this summary around, and grab a refresher next time you find your marketing message ineffective.

Here are some quick bookmarks from earlier:

Want a refresher on the 3 levels of problems? (Chapter 5)

Need to integrate your BrandScript into your website? (Chapter 12)

Need to incite action through pain avoidance? (Chapter 9)

Also don't forget to grab the SB7 formula cheatsheet here:

http://mindsetwarrior.com/sb7-formula-opt

BONUS:

Biases cloud our decision making on a day-to-day basis. You may have learned about a few of our cognitive biases back in your college or high school psychology class. It is time we get a refresher and understand how cognitive biases truly color our daily lives.

While we can't completely escape our biases, having an understanding of them can give us an advantage.

Get the FREE Cognitive Bias Report:

http://bit.ly/MWCogBiasReport

FEEDBACK:

If you'd like to provide feedback on how I can better improve these books, your opinion would be very much appreciated. Please send me an email at: summaries@mindsetwarrior.com I would love to hear from you.

- Alexa Taylor (The Mindset Warrior)

Made in the USA
Middletown, DE
19 February 2020